89 Juice and Meal Recipe Solutions for Common Fevers:

Give Your Body the Proper Nutrients to Recover From Common Fevers

By

Joe Correa CSN

COPYRIGHT

© 2019 Live Stronger Faster Inc.

All rights reserved

Reproduction or translation of any part of this work beyond that permitted by section 107 or 108 of the 1976 United States Copyright Act without the permission of the copyright owner is unlawful.

This publication is designed to provide accurate and authoritative information in regard to the subject matter covered. It is sold with the understanding that neither the author nor the publisher is engaged in rendering medical advice. If medical advice or assistance is needed, consult with a doctor. This book is considered a guide and should not be used in any way detrimental to your health. Consult with a physician before starting this nutritional plan to make sure it's right for you.

ACKNOWLEDGEMENTS

This book is dedicated to my friends and family that have had mild or serious illnesses so that you may find a solution and make the necessary changes in your life.

89 Juice and Meal Recipe Solutions for Common Fevers:

Give Your Body the Proper Nutrients to Recover From Common Fevers

By

Joe Correa CSN

CONTENTS

Copyright

Acknowledgements

About The Author

Introduction

Commitment

89 Juice and Meal Recipe Solutions for Common Fevers: Give Your Body the Proper Nutrients to Recover From Common Fevers

Additional Titles from This Author

ABOUT THE AUTHOR

After years of Research, I honestly believe in the positive effects that proper nutrition can have over the body and mind. My knowledge and experience has helped me live healthier throughout the years and which I have shared with family and friends. The more you know about eating and drinking healthier, the sooner you will want to change your life and eating habits.

Nutrition is a key part in the process of being healthy and living longer so get started today. The first step is the most important and the most significant.

INTRODUCTION

89 Juice and Meal Recipe Solutions for Common Fevers: Give Your Body the Proper Nutrients to Recover From Common Fevers

By Joe Correa CSN

There is a strong correlation between our Western diet and vulnerability to common fevers. Over the last century, food industry practices have changed such that we are increasingly exposed to unhealthy foods without our knowledge or understanding.

Although it sounds scary, having a fever is actually a sign that your body is fighting some out of the ordinary condition. A fever can be recognized by an increase in body temperature which usually occurs after an illness or some other health issue. This uncomfortable condition usually goes away on its own after just a couple of days and shouldn't be a reason for concern unless the temperature reaches 103F.

As I said earlier, these common fever symptoms are harmless most of the time and shouldn't be a reason for concern. There are, however, some cases when you should visit a doctor. These include severe headaches which can't be cured with your standard painkillers, skin rashes, mental confusion, constant vomiting, or difficulty breathing.

There are plenty of over-the-counter medications which can help reduce the symptoms of a fever but in some cases, it's much better to leave your body to heal on its own. Getting plenty of rest and eating the rights foods can help your body boost its immune system and speed up the healing process. This way, you will give your body the opportunity to defend itself in the most natural way possible without eliminating natural mechanisms of defense.

Let this book serve as your guide to preventing and fighting common fevers and improving your overall health through a smarter diet. The recipes you will find in this cookbook will not only help fight fevers, but they will also help you build up your immunity and get rid of those usual winter symptoms.

Enjoy!

COMMITMENT

In order to improve my condition, I *(your name)*, commit to eating more of these foods on a daily basis and to exercise at least 30 minutes daily:

- Berries (especially blueberries), peaches, cherries, apples, apricots, oranges, lemon juice, grapefruit, tangerines, mandarins, pears, etc.
- Broccoli, spinach, collard greens, sweet potatoes, avocado, artichoke, baby corn, carrots, celery, cauliflower, onions, etc.
- Whole grains, steel-cut oats, oatmeal, quinoa, barley, etc.
- Black beans, red bean beans, garbanzo beans, lentils, etc.
- Nuts and seeds including: walnuts, cashews, flaxseeds, sesame seeds, etc.
- Fish
- 8 – 10 glasses of water

Sign here

X_____

89 JUICE AND MEAL RECIPE SOLUTIONS FOR COMMON FEVERS: GIVE YOUR BODY THE PROPER NUTRIENTS TO RECOVER FROM COMMON FEVERS

JUICES

1. Sweet Kale Avocado Juice

Ingredients:

1 cup fresh kale, torn

1 artichoke heart, chopped

1 cup avocado, cubed

1 large cucumber, sliced

1 cup green cabbage, torn

1 tbsp liquid honey

Preparation:

Using a sharp knife, trim off the outer leaves of the artichoke. Wash it and cut into small pieces. Set aside.

Peel the avocado and cut in half. Remove the pit and cut into cubes. Reserve the rest of the avocado for some other juice. Set aside.

Wash the cucumber and cut into thick slices. Set aside.

Wash the basil and cabbage thoroughly and torn with hands. Set aside.

Now, process artichoke, avocado, cucumber, basil, and cabbage in a juicer. Transfer to serving glasses and stir in the liquid honey.

Refrigerate for 30 minutes before serving.

Nutrition information per serving: Kcal: 379, Protein: 14.2g, Carbs: 73.6g, Fats: 22.8g

2. Peach Kiwi Juice

Ingredients:

5 medium-sized apricots, sliced

1 large peach, sliced

1 large kiwi, peeled

A bunch of fresh spinach, chopped

1 tbsp fresh mint, chopped

¼ cup of water

Preparation:

Wash the peach and cut in half. Remove the pit and cut into small pieces. Set aside.

Peel the kiwi and cut lengthwise in half. Set aside.

Wash the apricots and cut in half. Remove the pits and cut into chunks. Set aside.

Wash the spinach and mint under cold running water. Drain and roughly chop it. Set aside.

Now, combine peach, kiwi, apricots, spinach, and mint in a juicer and process until juiced.

Transfer to serving glasses and refrigerate before serving.

Nutrition information per serving: Kcal: 211, Protein: 2.8g, Carbs: 58.8g, Fats: 2.8g

3. Blueberry Strawberry Juice

Ingredients:

1 cup blueberries

1 cup strawberries

1 cup cranberries

1 cup raspberries

1 cup blackberries

1 small Granny Smith's apple

¼ cup water

1 tsp pure coconut sugar

2 oz of water

Preparation:

Combine all berries in a colander and rinse under cold running water. Cut the strawberries in half and set aside.

Soak the berries in water for 10 minutes. Drain and set aside.

Wash the apple and remove the core. Cut into bite-sized pieces and set aside.

Now, process all berries and apple in a juicer. Transfer to serving glasses and stir in the coconut sugar and water.

Add some ice and serve immediately.

Nutrition information per serving: Kcal: 210, Protein: 5.7g, Carbs: 82g, Fats: 2.4g

4. Cucumber Lemon Juice

Ingredients:

1 whole cucumber, sliced

1 large lemon, peeled

5 large plums, pitted and halved

1 cup purple cabbage, torn

1 cup beets, trimmed

2 oz water

Preparation:

Wash the cucumber and cut into thick slices. Set aside.

Peel the lemon and cut lengthwise in half. Set aside.

Wash the plums and cut in half. Remove the pits and cut into quarters. Set aside.

Wash the cabbage thoroughly under cold running water. Drain and torn with hands.

Wash the beets and trim off the green parts. Cut into bite-sized pieces and set aside.

Now, process cucumber, lemon, plums, cabbage, and beets in a juicer.

Transfer to serving glasses and add some ice before serving.

Enjoy!

Nutrition information per serving: Kcal: 243, Protein: 8.3g, Carbs: 73.6g, Fats: 1.7g

5. Lettuce Cauliflower Juice

Ingredients:

1 cup Iceberg lettuce, chopped

1 cup cauliflower, chopped

1 cup turnip greens, chopped

1 cup kale, chopped

1 large cucumber, sliced

Preparation:

Combine Iceberg lettuce, turnip greens, and kale in a colander and wash under cold running water. Drain and roughly chop it. Set aside.

Trim off the outer leaves of cauliflower. Wash it and cut into small pieces. Fill the measuring cup and reserve the rest for some other juice. Set aside.

Wash the cucumber and cut into thick slices. Set aside.

Now, combine Iceberg lettuce, turnip greens, kale, cauliflower, and cucumber in a juicer and process until juiced.

Transfer to serving glasses and add some ice before serving.

Enjoy!

Nutrition information per serving: Kcal: 96, Protein: 8.3g, Carbs: 27.6g, Fats: 1.6g

6. Apple Kale Juice

Ingredients:

1 large Honeycrisp apple, cored

1 cup fresh kale, chopped

1 medium-sized fennel bulb

1 cup of mustard greens, torn

1 large red bell pepper, seeded

1 tbsp liquid honey

Preparation:

Wash the apple and remove the core. Cut into bite-sized pieces and set aside.

Combine kale and mustard greens in a colander. Wash under cold running water and torn with hands. Set aside.

Wash the fennel bulb and trim off the wilted outer layers. Cut into small chunks and set aside.

Wash the bell pepper and cut in half. Remove the seeds and chop into small slices. Set aside.

Now, process fennel, apple, kale, mustard greens, and bell pepper in a juicer.

Transfer to serving glasses and stir in the honey.

Refrigerate for 10 minutes before serving.

Nutrition information per serving: Kcal: 258, Protein: 9.5g, Carbs: 88.4g, Fats: 3.2g

7. Spicy Watermelon Juice

Ingredients:

2 cups watermelon, seeded

1/8 tsp Jalapeno pepper, ground

1 cup Romaine lettuce, chopped

1 large orange, peeled

1 cup fresh broccoli, chopped

Preparation:

Cut the watermelon lengthwise. For two cups, you will need about two large wedges. Peel and cut into chunks. Remove the seeds and set aside. Reserve the rest of the melon for some other juices.

Combine lettuce and broccoli in a colander and rinse under cold running water. Drain and chop into small pieces. Set aside.

Peel the orange and divide into wedges. Set aside.

Now, process watermelon, lettuce, broccoli, and orange in a juicer.

Transfer to serving glasses and stir in the jalapeno pepper for some extra spicy flavor. Refrigerate for 10 minutes before serving.

Enjoy!

Nutrition information per serving: Kcal: 185, Protein: 5g, Carbs: 52.8g, Fats: 1.3g

8. Swiss Chard Cucumber Juice

Ingredients:

2 cups Swiss chard, torn

1 large cucumber, sliced

1 cup fresh parsley, torn

1 medium-sized Zestar apple, cored

1 small orange, peeled

Preparation:

Combine Swiss chard and parsley in a colander and wash thoroughly under cold running water. Drain and torn with hands. Set aside.

Wash the cucumber and cut into thick slices. Set aside.

Wash the apple and remove the core. Cut into bite-sized pieces and set aside.

Peel the orange and divide into wedges. Set aside.

Now, combine Swiss chard, parsley, cucumber, apple, and orange in a juicer and process until juiced. Transfer to serving glasses and add some ice before serving.

Enjoy!

Nutrition information per serving: Kcal: 161, Protein: 6.3g, Carbs: 46.3g, Fats: 1.2g

9. Raspberry Carrot Juice

Ingredients:

1 large grapefruit, peeled

1 cup raspberries

1 large carrot, sliced

1 medium-sized Granny Smith's apple, cored

1 small ginger root slice, 1-inch

1 oz water

Preparation:

Place the raspberries in a colander and rinse under cold running water. Drain and set aside.

Wash the carrot and cut into thick slices. Set aside.

Peel the grapefruit and divide into wedges. Set aside.

Wash the apple and remove the core. Cut into bite-sized pieces. Set aside.

Peel the ginger root and set aside.

Now, process raspberries, carrot, grapefruit, apple, and ginger in a juicer.

Transfer to serving glasses and stir in the water. Add few

ice cubes or refrigerate before serving.

Enjoy!

Nutrition information per serving: Kcal: 239, Protein: 4.9g, Carbs: 76.2g, Fats: 1.7g

10. Pomegranate Kale Juice

Ingredients:

1 cup pomegranate seeds

1 cup fresh kale, torn

1 large lemon, peeled

1 cup watercress, torn

1 cup Swiss chard, torn

1 bunch fresh spinach, torn

1 oz water

1 tsp agave nectar

Preparation:

Combine kale, watercress, Swiss chard, and spinach in a colander. Rinse thoroughly under cold running water. Drain and torn with hands. Set aside.

Cut the top of the pomegranate fruit using a sharp knife. Slice down to each of the white membranes inside of the fruit. Pop the seeds into a bowl and set aside.

Peel the lemon and cut lengthwise in half. Set aside.

Now, process, pomegranate seeds, lemon, kale, watercress, Swiss chard, and spinach in a juicer.

Transfer to serving glasses and add few ice cubes before serving.

Enjoy!

Nutrition information per serving: Kcal: 372, Protein: 12.1g, Carbs: 68.6g, Fats: 22.8g

11. Apple Cucumber Juice

Ingredients:

2 small green apples, cored

1 large cucumber, sliced

1 medium-sized carrot, sliced

1 large beet, trimmed

1 small ginger knob, 1 inch

Preparation:

Wash the apples and remove the core. Cut into bite-sized pieces and set aside.

Wash the cucumber and carrot. Cut into thick slices and set aside.

Wash the beet and trim off the green parts. Cut into small pieces and set aside.

Peel the ginger root knob and set aside.

Now, combine apple, cucumber, carrot, beet, and ginger in a juicer and process until juiced.

Transfer to serving glasses and add some ice cubes and serve immediately.

Enjoy!

Nutrition information per serving: Kcal: 166, Protein: 4.7g, Carbs: 48.4g, Fats: 0.9g

12. Watermelon Cranberries Juice

Ingredients:

1 cup watermelon, chopped

1 cup cranberries

1 large banana, sliced

1 whole kiwi, peeled

5 large strawberries, chopped

Preparation:

Cut the watermelon lengthwise. For one cup, you will need a large slice. Peel and cut into chunks. Remove the seeds and set aside. Reserve the rest for some other juices.

Rinse the cranberries thoroughly and slightly drain. Set aside.

Peel the banana and cut into thin slices. Set aside.

Peel the kiwi and cut lengthwise in half. Set aside.

Wash the strawberries and cut into bite-sized pieces. Set aside.

Now, combine watermelon, cranberries, banana, kiwi, and strawberries in a juicer and process until juiced.

Transfer to a serving glass and add some ice before serving.

Enjoy!

Nutritional information per serving: Kcal: 236, Protein: 4.3g, Carbs: 72.9g, Fats: 1.4g

13. Mandarin Orange Juice

Ingredients:

2 mandarin oranges, wedged

1 cup blueberries

1 cup cherries, pitted

1 cup green grapes

¼ tsp cinnamon, ground

Preparation:

Peel the mandarin oranges and divide into wedges. Set aside.

Combine blueberries and grapes in a colander and wash under cold running water. Slightly drain and set aside.

Wash the cherries and cut each in half. Remove the pits and set aside.

Now, combine oranges, blueberries, cherries, and grapes in a juicer and process until juiced.

Transfer to a serving glass and stir in the cinnamon.

Add some ice and serve immediately.

Nutritional information per serving: Kcal: 249, Protein: 4.2g, Carbs: 73.2g, Fats: 1.2g

14. Pomegranate Pear Juice

Ingredients:

1 cup pomegranate seeds

1 small pear, chopped

1 medium-sized orange, peeled

1 small zucchini, chopped

1 cup fresh mint, torn

1 tbsp liquid honey

Preparation:

Cut the top of the pomegranate fruit using a sharp paring knife. Slice down to each of the white membranes inside of the fruit. Pop the seeds into a measuring cup and set aside.

Wash the pear and cut in half. Remove the core and cut into bite-sized pieces. Set aside.

Peel the orange and divide into wedges. Cut each wedge in half and set aside.

Peel the zucchini and cut into small chunks. Set aside.

Rinse the mint under cold running water using a colander. Slightly drain and torn with hands. Set aside.

Now, combine pomegranate seeds, pear, orange, zucchini,

and mint in a juicer and process until juiced. Transfer to a serving glass and stir in the honey.

Add some crushed ice and serve immediately.

Nutritional information per serving: Kcal: 259, Protein: 5.6g, Carbs: 61.6g, Fats: 2.1g

15. Cranberry Watercress Juice

Ingredients:

2 large pears, chopped

1 cup cranberries

1 cup watercress, torn

½ cup fresh spinach, torn

1 small ginger knob, peeled

Preparation:

Place the cranberries in a colander and rinse thoroughly. Slightly drain and set aside.

Wash watercress and spinach thoroughly under cold running water. Drain and torn with hands. Set aside.

Wash the pears and cut in half. Remove the core and cut into bite-sized pieces. Set aside.

Peel the ginger and set aside.

Now, combine cranberries, watercress, pears, spinach, and ginger in a juicer and process until well juiced. Transfer to a serving glass and stir in some water if you like. However, it is optional.

Refrigerate for 10 minutes before serving.

Enjoy!

Nutritional information per serving: Kcal: 249, Protein: 3.8g, Carbs: 86.1g, Fats: 0.9g

16. Avocado Mango Juice

Ingredients:

1 cup avocado, chunked

1 cup mango, chopped

1 small zucchini, chopped

1 whole lime, peeled

1 oz coconut water

1 tsp fresh mint, finely chopped

Preparation:

Peel the avocado and cut in half. Remove the pit and cut into chunks. Set aside.

Wash and peel the mango. Chop into bite-sized pieces and set aside.

Peel the zucchini and cut lengthwise in half. Scrape out the seeds and wash it. Cut into small pieces and set aside.

Peel the lime and cut lengthwise in half. Set aside.

Now, combine avocado, mango, zucchini, lime, and mint in a juicer and process until juiced. Transfer to a serving glass and stir in the coconut water. Add some crushed ice and serve immediately.

Nutritional information per serving: Kcal: 309, Protein: 5.8g, Carbs: 44.5g, Fats: 22.4g

17. Grape Kiwi Juice

Ingredients:

1 cup green grapes

1 whole kiwi, peeled

1 cup watermelon, cubed

1 medium-sized pear, chopped

1 tsp agave nectar

Preparation:

Wash the grapes and set aside.

Peel the kiwi and cut lengthwise in half. Set aside.

Cut the watermelon lengthwise. Cut one large wedge and peel it. Cut into chunks and fill the measuring cup. Remove the seeds and set aside. Reserve the rest of the melon for some other juices.

Wash the pear and remove the core. Cut into bite-sized pieces and set aside.

Now, combine grapes, kiwi, watermelon, and pear in a juicer and process until well juiced.

Transfer to a serving glass and stir in the agave nectar. Add some crushed ice before serving.

Enjoy!

Nutritional information per serving: Kcal: 236, Protein: 3g, Carbs: 70.5g, Fats: 1.2g

18. Avocado Pomegranate Juice

Ingredients:

1 cup strawberries, chopped

1 cup avocado, cubed

1 pomegranate seeds

1 cup cucumber, sliced

1 medium-sized orange, wedged

Preparation:

Peel the avocado and cut in half. Remove the pit and cut into cubes. Fill the measuring cup and reserve the rest for later.

Cut the top of the pomegranate fruit using a sharp paring knife. Slice down to each of the white membranes inside of the fruit. Pop the seeds into a measuring cup and set aside.

Wash the strawberries and cut into small pieces. Set aside.

Wash the cucumber and cut into thin slices. Fill the measuring cup and reserve the rest for later.

Peel the orange and divide into wedges. Chop each wedge in half and set aside.

Now, combine avocado, pomegranate, strawberries,

cucumber, and orange in a juicer. Process until well juiced.

Transfer to a serving glass and add some crushed ice before serving.

Nutritional information per serving: Kcal: 335, Protein: 6.6g, Carbs: 53.2g, Fats: 23.5g

19. Cherry Lime Juice

Ingredients:

1 cup fresh cherries, pitted

1 whole lime, peeled

1 cup avocado, cubed

1 medium-sized orange, wedged

1 tbsp honey, raw

Preparation:

Wash the cherries and cut each in half. Remove the pits and set aside.

Peel the lime and cut lengthwise in half. Set aside.

Peel the avocado and cut in half. Remove the pit and cut into small cubes. Fill the measuring cup and reserve the rest for later.

Peel the orange and divide into wedges. Cut each wedge in half and set aside.

Now, combine cherries, lime, avocado, and orange in a juicer and process until well juiced. Transfer to a serving glass and stir in the honey.

Add some crushed ice and serve.

Nutritional information per serving: Kcal: 408, Protein: 6g, Carbs: 74.5g, Fats: 22.5g

20. Broccoli Apple Juice

Ingredients:

1 cup cauliflower, chopped

1 cup broccoli, chopped

1 small Granny Smith's apple, cored

1 cup fresh kale, torn

¼ tsp ginger, ground

Preparation:

Wash the broccoli thoroughly and chop into small pieces. Set aside.

Wash the apple and cut lengthwise in half. Remove the core and cut into bite-sized pieces. Set aside.

Wash the cauliflower and trim off the outer leaves. Cut into small pieces and set aside.

Rinse the kale under cold running water and slightly drain. Torn with hands and set aside.

Now, combine broccoli, apple, cauliflower, and kale in a juicer and process until well juiced. Transfer to a serving glass and stir in the ground ginger.

Refrigerate for 10-15 minutes before serving.

Nutritional information per serving: Kcal: 131, Protein: 8.1g, Carbs: 36.8g, Fats: 1.5g

21. Apple Mint Juice

Ingredients:

1 medium-sized Granny Smith's apple, cored

1 cup fresh mint, torn

2 cups Brussels sprouts, halved

1 cup fresh kale, torn

1 whole lime, peeled

1 oz water

Preparation:

Wash the apple and cut in half. Remove the core and cut into bite-sized pieces. Set aside.

Combine mint and kale in a large colander and rinse under cold running water. Slightly drain and torn with hands. Set aside.

Wash the Brussels sprouts and trim off the outer leaves. Cut in half and fill the measuring cup. Reserve the rest for later.

Peel the lime and cut lengthwise in half. Set aside.

Now, combine apple, mint, Brussels sprouts, kale, and lime in a juicer and process until juiced. Transfer to a serving glass and stir in the water.

Refrigerate for 5 minutes before serving.

Enjoy!

Nutritional information per serving: Kcal: 171, Protein: 10.6g, Carbs: 51.7g, Fats: 1.7g

22. Plum Lemon Juice

Ingredients:

2 medium-sized peaches, pitted

2 whole plums, pitted

1 whole lemon, peeled

1 cup watermelon

¼ tsp ginger, ground

Preparation:

Wash the plums and cut lengthwise in half. Remove the pits and set aside.

Peel the lemons and cut lengthwise in half. Set aside.

Wash the peaches and cut in half. Remove the pits and cut into bite-sized pieces. Set aside.

Cut the watermelon lengthwise. For one cup, you will need a large slice. Peel and cut into chunks. Remove the seeds and set aside. Reserve the rest for some other juices.

Now, combine plums, lemon, peaches, and watermelon in a juicer and process until juiced. Transfer to a serving glass and stir in the ginger. For some extra taste, add some freshly grated lemon zest. However, it's optional.

Refrigerate for 10 minutes before serving.

Nutritional information per serving: Kcal: 205, Protein: 5.2g, Carbs: 60.6g, Fats: 1.5g

23. Lemon Peach Juice

Ingredients:

1 whole lemon, peeled

1 large peach, pitted

1 large Zestar apple, cored

1 medium-sized carrot, chopped

¼ tsp cinnamon, ground

2 oz water

Preparation:

Peel the lemon and cut lengthwise in half. Set aside.

Wash the peach and cut in half. Remove the pit and cut into bite-sized pieces. Set aside.

Wash the apple and cut lengthwise in half. Remove the core and cut into bite-sized pieces. Set aside.

Wash and peel the carrot. Cut into small chunks and set aside.

Now, combine lemon, peach, apple, and carrot in a juicer. Process until nicely juiced. Transfer to a serving glass and stir in the water and cinnamon.

Add some ice or refrigerate for 5 minutes before serving.

Enjoy!

Nutritional information per serving: Kcal: 165, Protein: 3.6g, Carbs: 50.7g, Fats: 1.1g

24.   Mango Banana Juice

Ingredients:

1 cup mango, chunked

1 medium-sized banana, chopped

1 large guava, chopped

1 large orange, wedged

1 oz coconut water

Preparation:

Wash and peel the mango and guava. Cut into small chunks and set aside.

Peel the banana and cut into small chunks. Set aside.

Peel the orange and divide into wedges. Set aside.

Now, combine mango, banana, guava, and orange in a juicer and process until well juiced. Transfer to a serving glass and stir in the water.

Add some ice and serve immediately.

Enjoy!

Nutritional information per serving: Kcal: 275, Protein: 5.7g, Carbs: 81.1g, Fats: 1.8g

25. Broccoli Beet Greens Juice

Ingredients:

1 cup broccoli, chopped

1 cup beet greens, torn

1 cup fresh basil, torn

1 large lemon, peeled

1 medium-sized Honeycrisp apple, cored

1 cup cauliflower, chopped

Preparation:

Wash the broccoli and chop into small pieces. Set aside.

Combine beet greens and basil in a large colander. Rinse under cold running water and drain. Torn with hands and set aside.

Peel the lemon and cut lengthwise in half. Set aside.

Wash the apple and cut lengthwise in half. Remove the core and cut into bite-sized pieces. Set aside.

Trim off the outer leaves of a cauliflower. Wash it and fill and cut into small pieces. Fill the measuring cup and reserve the rest in the refrigerator.

Now, combine broccoli, beet greens, basil, lemon, apple,

and cauliflower in a juicer. Process until well juiced and transfer to a serving glass.

Add few ice cubes and serve immediately.

Nutritional information per serving: Kcal: 137, Protein: 7.3g, Carbs: 42.1g, Fats: 1.3g

26. Carrot Orange Juice

Ingredients:

2 large carrots, peeled and chopped

1 large orange, wedged

1 cup raspberries

¼ tsp ginger, ground

1 tbsp liquid honey

Preparation:

Wash the carrots and peel them. Cut into small chunks and set aside.

Peel the orange and divide into wedges. Set aside.

Using a colander, rinse the raspberries under cold running water and drain. Set aside.

Now, combine raspberries, carrots, and orange in a juicer and process until well juiced. Transfer to a serving glass and stir in the ginger and honey.

Refrigerate for 10 minutes before serving.

Nutritional information per serving: Kcal: 204, Protein: 4.5g, Carbs: 67.1g, Fats: 1.3g

27. Lemon Celery Juice

Ingredients:

1 large lemon, peeled

3 large celery stalks, chopped

1 large Granny Smith's apple, cored

1 large cucumber

2 oz coconut water

Preparation:

Peel the lemon and cut lengthwise in half. Set aside.

Wash the celery stalks and cut into small pieces. Set aside.

Wash the apple and cut lengthwise in half. Remove the core and cut into small chunks. Set aside.

Peel the cucumber and cut into small chunks. Set aside.

Now, combine lemon, celery, apple, and cucumber in a juicer and process until well juiced. Transfer to serving glasses and stir in the coconut water.

Add few ice cubes and serve immediately.

Enjoy!

Nutritional information per serving: Kcal: 175, Protein: 5.1g, Carbs: 50.2g, Fats: 1.3g

28. Spinach Lettuce Juice

Ingredients:

1 cup fresh spinach, torn

1 cup Iceberg lettuce, shredded

1 cup fresh coriander, chopped

1 whole cucumber, sliced

¼ tsp salt

Preparation:

Combine spinach, coriander, and lettuce in a large colander. Wash thoroughly under cold running water and slightly drain. Roughly chop all and set aside.

Wash the cucumber and cut into thin slices. Set aside.

Now, combine spinach, lettuce, coriander, and cucumber in a juicer and process until well juiced.

Transfer to a serving glass and stir in the salt. Optionally, add some ground pepper or even cayenne pepper for some spicy taste.

Serve immediately.

Nutrition information per serving: Kcal: 85, Protein: 10.3g, Carbs: 23.9g, Fats: 1.8g

29. Cabbage Beet Juice

Ingredients:

1 cup purple cabbage, torn

1 whole beet, chopped

1 cup broccoli, chopped

1 cup Swiss chard, torn

1 cup cucumber, sliced

¼ tsp turmeric, ground

Preparation:

Combine purple cabbage and Swiss chard in a large colander. Wash thoroughly under cold running water and slightly drain. Torn with hands and set aside.

Wash the beets and trim off the green parts. Cut into bite-sized pieces and set aside.

Wash the broccoli and trim off the outer layers. Chop it into small pieces and set aside.

Wash the cucumber and cut into thin slices. Fill the measuring cup and reserve the rest for later. Set aside.

Now, combine purple cabbage, beet, broccoli, Swiss chard, and cucumber in a juicer and process until juiced.

Transfer to a serving glass and stir in the turmeric. Refrigerate for 15 minutes and serve.

Enjoy!

Nutrition information per serving: Kcal: 79, Protein: 6.2g, Carbs: 23.7g, Fats: 0.8g

30. Lime Cucumber Juice

Ingredients:

1 whole lime, peeled

1 cup cucumber, sliced

2 medium-sized carrots, sliced

1 medium-sized orange, wedged

1 tbsp honey

Preparation:

Peel the lime and cut lengthwise in half. Set aside.

Wash the cucumber and cut into thin slices. Fill the measuring cup and reserve the rest for later.

Wash and peel the carrots. Cut into thin slices and set aside.

Peel the orange and divide into wedges. Cut each wedge in half and set aside.

Now, combine lime, cucumber, carrots, and orange in a juicer and process until juiced. Transfer to a serving glass and stir in the honey.

Add some ice before serving.

Enjoy!

Nutrition information per serving: Kcal: 163, Protein: 2.9g, Carbs: 32.6g, Fats: 0.6g

31. Red Orange Lemon Juice

Ingredients:

1 large red orange, peeled

1 whole lemon, peeled

1 medium-sized artichoke, chopped

1 whole lime, peeled

1 tbsp liquid honey

1 oz water

Preparation:

Peel the orange and divide into wedges. Cut each wedge in half and set aside.

Peel the lemon and lime. Cut each fruit lengthwise in half and set aside.

Trim off the outer layers of the artichoke using a sharp paring knife. Cut into bite-sized pieces and set aside.

Now, combine orange, lemon, artichoke, and lime in a juicer. Process until well juiced. Transfer to a serving glass and stir in the honey and water.

Refrigerate for 15 minutes before serving.

Nutrition information per serving: Kcal: 149, Protein: 5.9g, Carbs: 33.8g, Fats: 0.5g

32. Kale Lime Juice

Ingredients:

1 cup cauliflower, chopped

1 cup fresh kale, chopped

1 whole lime, peeled

1 cup cucumber, sliced

1 tsp agave nectar

Preparation:

Wash the kale thoroughly under cold running water and slightly drain. Chop into small pieces and set aside.

Peel the lime and cut lengthwise in half. Set aside.

Trim off the outer layer of the cauliflower. Cut into bite-sized pieces and wash it. Fill the measuring cup and sprinkle with some salt. Set aside.

Wash the cucumber and cut into thin slices. Fill the measuring cup and reserve the rest for some other juice. Set aside.

Now, combine kale, lime, cauliflower, and cucumber in a juicer. Process until well juiced. Transfer to a serving glass and stir in the agave nectar.

Refrigerate before serving.

Enjoy!

Nutrition information per serving: Kcal: 107, Protein: 11.4g, Carbs: 30.4g, Fats: 1.8g

33. Kiwi Peach Juice

Ingredients:

1 small apple, cored

1 whole kiwi, peeled

1 small peach, pitted

½ cup fresh spinach, torn

Preparation:

Peel the kiwi and cut lengthwise in half. Set aside.

Wash the peach and cut in half. Remove the pit and cut into bite-sized pieces. Set aside.

Wash the apple and cut in half. Remove the core and cut into bite-sized pieces. Set aside.

Rinse the spinach under cold running water and slightly drain. Torn with hands and set aside.

Now, combine kiwi, peach, apple, and spinach in a juicer and process until juiced. Transfer to a serving glass and add some ice.

Serve immediately.

Nutrition information per serving: Kcal: 165, Protein: 6.9g, Carbs: 47.6g, Fats: 1.5g

34. Cranberry Raspberry Juice

Ingredients:

1 cup of raspberries

1 cup of fresh mint, torn

1 cup of cranberries

1 whole lemon, peeled

1 medium-sized Zestar apple, cored

¼ tsp cinnamon, ground

Preparation:

Combine raspberries and cranberries in a large colander. Rinse thoroughly under cold running water and slightly drain. Set aside.

Rinse the mint and torn with hands. Set aside.

Peel the lemon and cut lengthwise in half. Set aside.

Wash the apple and cut in half. Remove the core and cut into bite-sized pieces.

Now, combine raspberries, mint, cranberries, lemon, and apple in a juicer and process until juiced. Transfer to a serving glass and stir in the cinnamon. Add some ice before serving.

Enjoy!

Nutrition information per serving: Kcal: 143, Protein: 3.8g, Carbs: 53.5g, Fats: 1.5g

35. Tropical Orange Juice

Ingredients:

1 medium-sized orange, peeled

1 large carrot, sliced

1 whole guava, peeled

1 whole lemon, peeled

1 tbsp liquid honey

Preparation:

Peel the orange and divide into wedges. Cut each wedge in half and set aside.

Wash and peel the carrot. Cut into thin slices and set aside.

Peel the guava with a sharp paring knife. Cut into small chunks and set aside.

Peel the lemon and cut lengthwise in half. Set aside.

Now, combine orange, carrot, guava, and lemon in a juicer and process until juiced. Transfer to a serving glass and stir in the honey.

Add some ice and serve immediately.

Nutrition information per serving: Kcal: 168, Protein: 3.9g, Carbs: 35.6g, Fats: 1.1g

36. Mango Pear Juice

Ingredients:

1 medium-sized pear, chopped

1 cup pomegranate seeds

1 cup mango, chunked

1 cup Iceberg lettuce, shredded

1 tbsp liquid honey

1 oz water

Preparation:

Wash the pear and cut into small pieces. Set aside.

Cut the top of the pomegranate fruit using a sharp paring knife. Slice down to each of the white membranes inside of the fruit. Pop the seeds into a measuring cup and set aside.

Peel the mango and cut into small chunks. Fill the measuring cup and reserve the rest in the refrigerator. Set aside.

Wash the lettuce thoroughly under cold running water and shred it. Fill the measuring cup and reserve the rest for later.

Now, combine pear, pomegranate, mango, and lettuce in a

juicer and process until well juiced. Transfer to a serving glass and stir in the honey and water. Add some ice and serve immediately.

Nutrition information per serving: Kcal: 230, Protein: 4.1g, Carbs: 69.6g, Fats: 2.1g

37. Cherry Ginger Juice

Ingredients:

1 cup cherries, pitted

1 small ginger slice, peeled

1 cup apricots, pitted

1 oz of coconut water

Preparation:

Wash the cherries and remove the stems, if any. Cut each in half and remove the pits. Fill the measuring cup and set aside.

Peel the ginger slice and set aside.

Wash the apricots and cut in half. Remove the pits and cut into small pieces. Fill the measuring cup and set aside.

Now, combine cherries, ginger, and apricots in a juicer and process until well juiced. Transfer to a serving glass and stir in the coconut water. For a sweeter taste, add some honey. However, it's optional.

Refrigerate for 15 minutes before serving.

Enjoy!

Nutrition information per serving: Kcal: 149, Protein: 3.8g, Carbs: 40.8g, Fats: 0.9g

38.   Plum Apple Juice

Ingredients:

2 whole plums, chopped

1 medium-sized Granny Smith's apple, cored

1 cup avocado, cubed

1 whole lemon, peeled

¼ tsp cinnamon, ground

1 tbsp coconut water

Preparation:

Wash the plums and cut lengthwise in half. Remove the pits and cut into bite-sized pieces. Set aside.

Wash the apple and cut in half. Remove the pit and cut into small pieces. Set aside.

Peel the avocado and cut in half. Remove the pit and cut into small cubes. Fill the measuring cup and reserve the rest for later.

Peel the lemon and cut into half. Set aside.

Now, combine avocado, plums, apple, and lemon in a juicer and process until juiced. Transfer to a serving glass and stir in the cinnamon and coconut water.

Refrigerate for 10 minutes before serving.

Enjoy!

Nutrition information per serving: Kcal: 341, Protein: 5.3g, Carbs: 56.1g, Fats: 22.8g

39. Grape Apple Juice

Ingredients:

1 cup black grapes

1 small Golden Delicious apple, cored

1 cup cranberries

¼ tsp cinnamon, ground

Preparation:

Wash the grapes and fill the measuring cup. Reserve the rest for later.

Wash the apple and cut in half. Remove the core and cut into bite-sized pieces. Set aside.

Rinse the cranberries using a colander. Slightly drain and set aside.

Now, combine grapes, apple, and cranberries in a juicer and process until juiced. Transfer to a serving glass and stir in the cinnamon.

Add some ice before serving and enjoy!

Nutritional information per serving: Kcal: 190, Protein: 2.1g, Carbs: 56.7g, Fats: 1.1g

40. Pear Blueberry Juice

Ingredients:

1 medium-sized pear, chopped

1 cup blueberries

1 whole lemon, peeled

½ cup strawberries, sliced

1 small ginger knob, peeled

1 oz water

Preparation:

Wash the pear and cut in half. Remove the core and cut into small pieces. Set aside.

Rinse the blueberries and fill the measuring cup. Set aside.

Peel the lemon and cut in half. Set aside.

Wash the strawberries and remove the stems. Cut into small pieces and fill the measuring cup. Set aside.

Peel the ginger knob and set aside.

Now, combine pear, blueberries, lemon, strawberries, and ginger in a juicer and process until juiced. Transfer to a serving glass and stir in the water.

Serve cold.

Nutritional information per serving: Kcal: 143, Protein: 2.4g, Carbs: 52.7g, Fats: 0.8g

41. Banana Cinnamon Juice

Ingredients:

1 large banana, peeled

¼ tsp cinnamon, ground

1 medium-sized watermelon wedge

1 whole lime, peeled

1 small Granny Smith's apple, cored

Preparation:

Peel the banana and chop into small chunks. Set aside.

Cut one large watermelon wedge and peel it. Remove the seeds and cut into bite-sized pieces. Wrap the rest of the melon in a plastic foil and refrigerate.

Peel the lime and cut lengthwise in half. Set aside.

Wash the apple and cut in half. Remove the core and cut into bite-sized pieces. Set aside.

Now, combine banana melon, lime, and apple in a juicer and process until juiced. Transfer to a serving glass and stir in the cinnamon.

Refrigerate for 15 minutes before serving.

Nutritional information per serving: Kcal: 226, Protein: 4.6g, Carbs: 29.4g, Fats: 1.2g

42. Green Kiwi Spinach Juice

Ingredients:

1 whole kiwi, peeled

1 cup fresh spinach, chopped

1 cup mango, chunked

1 small ginger knob, peeled

2 tbsp coconut water

Preparation:

Peel the kiwi and cut lengthwise in half. Set aside.

Wash the spinach thoroughly under cold running water. Slightly drain and chop it into small pieces. Set aside.

Peel the mango and cut into small chunks. Fill the measuring cup and reserve the rest in the refrigerator.

Peel the ginger knob and set aside.

Now, combine kiwi, spinach, mango, and ginger in a juicer and process until juiced. Transfer to a serving glass and stir in the coconut water. Refrigerate for 10 minutes before serving.

Enjoy!

Nutritional information per serving: Kcal: 190, Protein: 9.1g, Carbs: 53.6g, Fats: 2.2g

MEALS

1. Italian pasta

Ingredients:

2 cups of buckwheat pasta

1 cup of cottage cheese

1 cup of red peppers, chopped

1 tbsp of Parmesan cheese

4 tbsp of Greek yogurt

Preparation:

Use package directions to boil pasta. Drain well and let it stand.

Meanwhile, combine red peppers, Parmesan cheese and Greek yogurt in a saucepan. Let it melt over a medium temperature and add cottage cheese. Stir fry for 5 minutes.

Pour the shrimp sauce over pasta and serve warm.

Nutrition information per serving: Kcal: 242 Protein: 13.4g, Carbs: 31.4g, Fats: 7.1g

2. Potato and cheese

Ingredients:

3 medium sweet potatoes

½ cup of cottage cheese

¼ cup of cheddar cheese

¼ cup of organic tomato puree

¼ cup parsley, chopped

Preparation:

Preheat the oven to 350 degrees. Wash and peel the potatoes. Cut each potato into 2 slices and bake for 30 minutes. Remove from the oven.

Combine cottage and cheddar cheese in a bowl and spread over potato slices. Allow it to melt slightly. Top with tomato puree and chopped parsley. Serve immediately.

Nutrition information per serving: Kcal: 220 Protein: 4.2g, Carbs: 40.4g, Fats: 4.7g

3. Mushroom sliders

Ingredients:

1 sweet potato

1 cup of fresh button mushrooms

1 cup of cottage cheese

3 egg whites

¾ cup of chia seeds

¾ of a cup of long grain rice

1 tsp of tarragon

1 tsp of parsley

1 tsp of garlic powder

1 cup of chopped spinach

Preparation:

Pour 1 cup of water in a small saucepan. Bring it to boil and cook rice until it's slightly sticky. This should take about 10 minutes. At the same time, cook chia seeds until soft in a separate pot. Finely chop mushrooms. Thoroughly rinse spinach. Mix all the ingredients together in a large bowl. Put the bowl into the fridge to chill for 15 to 30 minutes. Take mixture out of the fridge and form into patties. Make sure cooking surfaces are cleaned and greased before adding patties to prevent them from sticking. Fry each piece on a medium temperature for about 5 minutes on both side.

Nutrition information per serving: Kcal: 300 Protein: 10g, Carbs: 51.4g, Fats: 6.1g

4. Barbecue peas

Ingredients:

2 cups of rice, washed and rinsed

5 cups of water

½ cup of non-fat yogurt

½ cup of Greek yogurt

2 tbsp of brown sugar

1 tbsp of vinegar

1 tsp of mustard

1 tsp of Worcestershire sauce

2 tsp of tomato sauce

1 small chopped onion

Preparation:

Preheat your oven at 350 degrees. Pour rice in water, and bring it to boil. Let it boil for 15 minutes, or until tender. Add all the ingredients to the boiled and tender rice, and stir the mixture to combine them well. Pour the rice in a baking dish an and bake for 45 minutes. Top with Greek yogurt.

Nutrition information per serving: Kcal: 110 Protein: 4,3g, Carbs: 15.6g, Fats: 2.2g

5. Buckwheat pasta with mozzarella

Ingredients:

1 small pack of buckwheat pasta

½ cup of chia seeds powder

1 small can of sugar-free tomato sauce

1 small mozzarella

1 tsp of rosemary

olive oil

salt

Preparation:

Use package instructions to cook pasta. Wash it and drain. Chop mozzarella into small pieces and mix with tomato sauce. Add chia seeds powder to this mixture. Cook this sauce for about 10 minutes, stirring constantly. Add rosemary, olive oil and salt. Cook for another 4-5 minutes and pour over pasta.

Nutrition information per serving: Kcal: 220 Protein: 8g, Carbs: 52.3g, Fats: 2.4g

6. Rice and mushroom mix

Ingredients:

2 cups of button mushrooms, sliced

1 cup of rice, cooked

½ cup of onions, chopped

1 tbsp of fresh celery, chopped

¼ cup of apple vinegar

4 tbsp of sea salt

5 tbsp of extra virgin olive oil

1/3 cup of toasted almonds

1/3 cup of sliced dried figs

Preparation:

In a medium sized bowl, combine the onions with apple vinegar and let it stand for about 10-15 minutes. Add salt and 2 tbsp of olive oil.

Meanwhile, heat up the olive oil in a large saucepan and add the mushrooms. Cook for few minutes, stirring constantly. Remove from the heat when the mushrooms release their water. Add rice, celery, figs and almonds to the saucepan. Mix well with mushrooms. Fry for several more minutes and remove from heat.

Pour the onion marinade on top and serve.

Nutrition information per serving: Kcal: 260 Protein: 6.4g, Carbs: 47.5g, Fats: 1g

7. Chia seeds with curry & fresh lime

Ingredients:

3 tsp of vegetable oil

2 tbsp of ginger, freshly grated

2 cloves of garlic, minced

3 carrots, chopped

1 large sweet potato, chopped

1 small onion, chopped

1 cup of dry chia seeds

4 cups of vegetable broth

1 tsp of curry powder

¾ tsp of salt

¼ tsp of pepper

lime wedges for serving

Preparation:

Heat oil in large saucepan over medium heat. Add the ginger, garlic, chopped carrots, potato, and onions. Saute' until vegetables become soft. Add the chia seeds, broth, and seasonings, stirring well while turning up the heat to medium high until mixture comes to a boil. Cover, turn heat back down to medium-low and simmer for 15 to 20 minutes, stirring occasionally, until seeds are tender and most of the liquid is absorbed. Serve with fresh lime wedges.

Nutrition information per serving: Kcal: 318 Protein: 32.5g, Carbs: 14g, Fats: 18.4g

8. Colorful plate

Ingredients:

1 cup of chopped red peppers

4 eggs

1 tbsp of minced macadamia nut

1 small tomato

1 tbsp of olive oil

1 tsp of vinegar

salt to taste

Preparation:

Boil the eggs for about 10 minutes. Remove from the water and allow it to cool. Peel and chop into small cubes. Mix with the other ingredients and season with olive oil, vinegar and salt. Keep in the fridge for 20 minutes before serving.

Nutrition information per serving: Kcal: 327 Protein: 23.5g, Carbs: 8.7 g, Fats: 23.5g

9. Cottage cheese with eggs

Ingredients:

2 cups of cottage cheese

2 tbsp of low fat cream

3 boiled egg

1 cup of chopped lettuce

1 cup of chopped cucumber

1 tsp of mint

1 tbsp of almond oil

salt to taste

Preparation:

Mash the egg and mix it with cheese and cream until smooth mixture. You can use electric mixer for this. Combine this mixture with chopped lettuce and cucumber, season with oil and salt. Sprinkle some mint on top. Serve cold.

Nutrition information per serving: Kcal: 84 Protein: 12.6g, Carbs: 3.7g, Fats: 1.2g

10. Walnut pastry

Ingredients:

1 tbsp of honey

½ cup of ground walnuts

2 cups of almond flour

1 tbsp of vanilla extract

3 large eggs

5 egg whites

½ tsp of sea salt

1 teaspoon of baking soda

2 tbsp of coconut oil

Preparation:

Put the honey, eggs, egg whites, walnuts and vanilla extract in the food processor and mix well for 40 seconds.

Pour the mixture in a bowl and add flour, baking soda and salt. Stir well with a fork or even better with an electric stick mixer to get a smooth dough.

Pour the coconut oil over a baking sheet. Preheat the oven to 250 degrees. It takes about 40 minutes for bread to start rising. When it does, remove it from the oven and let it stand for at least 2 hours before eating.

This bread is high in proteins and very good alternative to your regular bread.

Nutrition information per serving: Kcal: 155 Protein: 9.6g, Carbs: 26.2g, Fats: 2.2g

11. Green pepper eggs

Ingredients:

2 whole eggs

2 egg whites

2 small green peppers, chopped

¼ tsp of red pepper

¼ tsp of sea salt

1 tbsp of olive oil

Preparation:

Beat the eggs and egg whites with a fork. Season the eggs with red pepper and sea salt.

Heat up the olive oil over to medium-high heat and fry the chopped green peppers for about 10 minutes. Add eggs, stir well and fry for another 3 minutes. Remove from the heat and serve.

Nutrition information per serving: Kcal: 165 Protein: 13.4g, Carbs: 2.5g, Fats: 11.9g

12. Greek almond salad

Ingredients:

4 eggs, boiled

½ cup of grated almonds

1 large cucumber, cut into small cubes

1 cup of cherry tomatoes

1 cup of Greek yogurt

1 tbsp of lemon juice

1 tbsp of flaxseed oil

salt to taste

Preparation:

Mash the eggs in a large bowl, with a fork. Pour the Greek yogurt and mix well. Add cucumber and cherry tomatoes and leave in the fridge for at least 30 minutes. Remove from the fridge, add grated almonds and season with lemon juice, flaxseed oil and salt.

Nutrition information per serving: Kcal: 460 Protein: 15.4g, Carbs: 40.2g, Fats: 31g

13. Lemon cheese mix

Ingredients:

1 cup of chopped lettuce

1 cup of cottage cheese

¼ cup of lemon juice

1 tsp of ground garlic

salt to taste

Preparation:

Combine the ingredients in a large bowl. Keep in the fridge for at least 30 minutes. You can add some pepper, but that is optional.

Nutrition information per serving: Kcal: 92 Protein: 5g, Carbs: 11.1g, Fats: 3.2g

14. Avocado rice

Ingredients

1 cup of gorgonzola cheese

1 medium avocado, ripe

1 ½ cup of cooked brown rice

2 eggs

1 tbsp of honey

2 tsp of olive oil

¼ tsp of red pepper

1 tbsp of red wine vinegar

2 tbsp of sesame seeds

1 cup of red beans

Preparation:

Heat up the olive oil in a large saucepan over a medium temperature. Add honey and stir well until it melts. Now add the gorgonzola and fry well for few minutes on each side. Season with pepper and remove from the saucepan. Use the same saucepan to fry eggs for about 2 minutes. Transfer to a plate and cut into strips.

In a small bowl, combine the rice with red wine vinegar and

red beans. Top with egg strips, shrimps and avocado slices.

Nutrition information per serving: Kcal: 330 Protein: 6.9g, Carbs: 34.7g, Fats: 21.4g

15. Orange eggplant

Ingredients:

2 eggplants, cut into half

½ cup of vegetable broth

2 tbsp of dry parsley, chopped

2 tbsp of walnuts, minced

½ cup of fresh orange juice

¼ tsp of orange zest

2 tsp of rice flour

½ tsp of sea salt

¼ tsp of black pepper

2 tbsp of olive oil

1 medium onion, chopped

1 cup of brown rice, cooked

Preparation:

Combine parsley, walnuts and orange zest in a bowl. Wash and pat dry the eggplant halves. Dust with the flour, salt and pepper.

Use a large saucepan to heat up the olive oil over a medium

temperature. Add the chopped onion and fry for about 3-4 minutes. Stir well and add the eggplant. Fry until golden color.

Now pour the vegetable broth and orange juice over the eggplant. Cover and let it cook for about 15 minutes on a very low temperature. Stir in the parsley mixture and remove from the heat. Serve warm.

Nutrition information per serving: Kcal: 430 Protein: 14.4g, Carbs: 63g, Fats: 14.7g

16. Spinach pizza

Ingredients:

1 medium pizza crust

¼ cup of tomato pizza sauce

½ cup of chopped spinach

½ small onion, chopped

1 cup of cottage cheese

½ cup of button mushrooms, sliced

¼ cup of ricotta, skim

2 tbsp of grated parmesan cheese

1 tbsp of olive oil

Preparation:

Preheat the oven to 350 degrees. Lay the pizza crust on a baking sheet. Spread the sauce over the pizza crust. Now add the spinach and the onions. Sprinkle with cottage cheese and mushrooms and make a final layer with ricotta and parmesan. Drizzle the olive oil.

Bake for about 10 minutes, cut and serve.

Nutrition information per serving: Kcal: 310 Protein: 12.4g, Carbs: 42g, Fats: 10.8g

17. Broccoli and ricotta pasta

Ingredients:

1 cup of whole wheat, gluten-free pasta

1 cup of cooked broccoli

¼ cup of skim ricotta

1 cup of chopped lean sausages

2 tbsp of parmesan cheese, grated

¼ tsp of salt

2 tbsp of olive oil

1 small onion, sliced

1 clove of garlic, ground

1/2 medium red onion, thinly sliced

1 garlic clove, sliced

Small pinch crushed red pepper flakes

2 tablespoons tomato paste

Preparation:

Pour 3 cups of water in a large pot. Bring it to boil and add broccoli. Cook for about 10 minutes until soft. Remove from the water and allow it to cool. Chop into bite-size pieces.

Now add the pasta into the same pot and use a package instructions to cook it.

Meanwhile, heat the olive oil in a large saucepan, over a medium temperature. Add the chopped sausages, onion slices, garlic, and red pepper. Cook for about 8 minutes, stiring occasionally. Add cooked broccoli and mix well until tender. Pour in the tomato sauce and cook for another minute.

Reduce heat to minimum and add pasta. Add some water if the mixture seems dry. Stir in skim ricotta and parmesan cheese. Serve warm.

Nutrition information per serving: Kcal: 536 Protein: 30.6g, Carbs: 74.2g, Fats: 13.5g

18. Feta frittata

Ingredients:

2 cups of chopped kale

3 tbsp of olive oil

1 medium eggplant, sliced

1 small onion, peeled and sliced

6 eggs, lightly beaten

½ cup of feta cheese

¼ tsp of salt

Preparation:

Boil kale for about 5 minutes. Drain and squeeze out as much liquid as possible. Slice roughly.

Heat up the olive oil in a large saucepan. Fry eggplant slices for about 3 minutes, turning often. Add onions and fry for another 2-3 minutes. Add kale and stir well. Season with salt. Pour over the beaten eggs, mix with a fork and remove from heat after about a minute.

Crumble feta cheese on top and serve warm.

Nutrition information per serving: Kcal: 207 Protein: 12.6g, Carbs: 3.4g, Fats: 16.4g

19. Crustless quiche

Ingredients:

1 small onion, chopped

4 eggs

1 tbsp of dry parsley, chopped

¼ cup of rice flour

1 tbsp of almond butter

2 cups of skim milk

½ tsp of salt

¼ tsp of pepper

Preparation:

In a large bowl, whisk together eggs and milk. Add rice flour and butter. Mix well with an electric mixer. Add other ingredients and pour this mixture into a baking dish.

Preheat oven to 300 degrees and bake for about 30 minutes.

Nutrition information per serving: Kcal: 250 Protein: 6g, Carbs: 4g, Fats: 22g

20. Mixed vegetable salad

Ingredients:

1 medium tomato

1 medium onion

1 cup of chopped lettuce

1 cup of chopped spinach

½ cup of chopped ruccola

1 small red pepper

½ cup of grated cabbage

1 cup of cottage cheese

2 tbsp of sunflower oil

1 tbsp of apple vinegar

salt to taste

Preparation:

This recipe is very easy to prepare and it takes about 10 minutes. All you want to do is combine the vegetables in a large bowl and mix well. Season with oil and vinegar. Salt to taste.

Nutrition information per serving: Kcal: 82 Protein: 5.3g, Carbs: 17.3g, Fats: 0.9g

21. Chia seeds bread

Ingredients:

3 cups of buckwheat flour

½ cup of canned pumpkin puree

1 cup of minced chia seeds

warm water

salt

½ pack of dry yeast

Preparation:

Mix flour, canned pumpkin puree and chia seeds with salt and yeast. Add warm water and stir until smooth dough. Let it stand in a warm place for about 30-40 minutes. Sprinkle with cold water and bake in preheated oven, at 350 degrees for about 40 minutes, until nice gold brown color. Remove from the oven, cover with a kitchen napkin and allow it to cool.

Nutrition information per serving: Kcal: 242 Protein: 13.4g, Carbs: 31.4g, Fats: 7.1g

22. Apple salad recipe

Ingredients:

1 large apple

1 cup of chopped spinach

1.5 cup of cream

1 tbsp of apple juice

½ cup of cherry tomatoes

1 tsp of apple vinegar

Preparation:

Wash and peel the apple. Cut it into thin slices. Use a large bowl to combine the apple with other ingredients. Season with apple vinegar and serve cold.

Nutrition information per serving: Kcal: 242 Protein: 2.2g, Carbs: 15.3g, Fats: 21g

23. Blue Stilton omelet

Ingredients:

½ cup of pureed prunes

1 cup of baby spinach leaves, chopped

1 tbsp of onion powder

¼ tsp of ground red pepper

¼ tsp of sea salt

½ cup of blue stiltoncheese

1 tbsp of flaxseed oil

milk, optional

Preparation:

Combine pureed prunes with baby spinach leaves and cheese. Beat well with a fork. Season with onion powder, red pepper and sea salt.

If your mixture is too thick, you can add some milk.

Heat up the olive oil over a medium heat. Add egg mixture and fry for 2-3 minutes.

Spread this mixture over a baking sheet and bake for another 15-20 minutes at 200 degrees.

Nutrition information per serving: Kcal: 120 Protein: 9.5g, Carbs: 6g, Fats: 9g

24. Side rolls

Ingredients:

1 cup rice flour

3 cups buckwheat flour

¼ cup melted butter

1 ½ cups warm water (176 °F)

1 tbsp of salt

2 tbsp of sugar

2 tbsp of olive oil

1 tablespoon of active dry yeast

Preparation:

Apply oil to a pan or bowl lightly, and put it aside. In another bowl, mix the rice flour, water, yeast, salt, sugar and oil and stir completely.

Add buckwheat flour to the mixture, ½ cup at a time, till the dough is elastic and soft enough to knead. Line your countertop, or any clean surface, with flour and knead the dough on top of it. Then cover the dough and leave it at room temperature for proofing.

When this is done, punch the dough, and make little rolls

out of it, adding a little amount of flour to them. Put these rolls on the pan that you prepared initially, and put them in a preheated oven (375 °F). Bake for 15 minutes, brush melted butter on the rolls and leave them to bake for another 5 minutes. This recipe will yield approximately 15 servings.

Nutrition information per serving: Kcal: 339 Protein: 25g, Carbs: 28.4g, Fats: 7.1g

25. Carrot cake

Ingredients:

1 ½ cups of tapioca flour

2 cups of rice flour

2 teaspoons vanilla

3 eggs

2 cups of sugar

1 ½ cups of vegetable oil

2 cups grated raw carrots

½ teaspoon salt

1 teaspoon active dry yeast

3 teaspoons cinnamon

1 cup of chopped walnuts

1 cup crushed and drained pineapples

Preparation:

Take a large bowl and place the tapioca flour in it. Add the vanilla, eggs, sugar and oil, mixing them well. Add the carrots, pineapples and walnuts to the mixture and fold them in. Combine the yeast, cinnamon, salt and rice flour in a separate bowl, mixing them to form a mixture. Next, combine all the ingredients, mixing the wet and dry ingredients.

Preheat the oven to 350 degrees. Take a baking pan and sprinkle flour on the bottom. Spread the dough on the pan and put it in the oven. Bake for 45 minutes. Cool the cake down before adding any frosting you prefer.

Nutrition information per serving: Kcal: 326 Protein: 3.4g, Carbs: 42.4g, Fats: 17.1g

26. Pepper biscuits

Ingredients:

1 teaspoon of salt

1 tablespoon of sugar

1 ½ cup of tapioca flour

1 teaspoon of active dry yeast

1 cupof milk

1 cup of buckwheat flour

Preparation:

Use a pastry blender to blend the ingredients. Once it is blended, start kneading the mixture. Roll it out flat to leave thickness at ½ inch. Cut the dough in half and place one half on top of the other. Roll the dough again, repeating the process 8 times.

Use a cookie cutter to cut the biscuits out and place them on a cookie sheet. Do NOT grease the cookie sheet. Brush the biscuit molds with oil and keep them for 30 minutes. For quick baking, set the heat at 450 degrees and bake for around 12 minutes. Or else, you can bake for 30 minutes at 375 degrees. This recipe allows you to make 8 biscuits at a time.

Nutrition information per serving: Kcal: 115 Protein: 20g, Carbs: 2g, Fats: 4g

27. Brussel sprouts chips

Ingredients:

1 pound of brussel sprouts (cleaned and washed)

3 teaspoons of honey

1 teaspoon of tomato sauce

2 tablespoons of ghee (can use almond butter instead)

½ teaspoon of chili paste (sweet)

½ teaspoon of lemon juice

¼ teaspoon of sesame oil

1 teaspoon of sesame seeds

salt to taste

pepper to taste

Preparation:

Set your oven to preheat at 350oF. Line two baking trays with baking paper and set aside. Cut the bottoms of the brussel sprouts and peel off all the leaves until you reach the heart. Set the heart aside. Take a bowl and combine the honey, chili paste, tomato sauce, sesame oil, lemon juice and the sesame seeds with the help of a whisk to combine well and set aside.

Place the brussel sprout leaves, all of them, into a large bowl and cover them with some ghee, salt and pepper until they are all coated. Take the baking trays and place the brussel leaves on them, making sure to separate the leaves evenly on the sheets. Pop into the oven and let them bake for 8 to 10 minutes or until they start to crisp and turn brown at the edges. Let them cool slightly before serving.

Nutrition information per serving: Kcal: 160 Protein: 7.6g, Carbs: 12.3g, Fats: 4g

28. Stuffed mushrooms

Ingredients:

16 button mushrooms, large, cleaned, de-stemmed mushroom stems, from the mushrooms, chopped finely

2 cloves of garlic, chopped finely

3 tablespoons of olive oil

2 shallots, whole, chopped finely

1 sweet paprika

salt to taste

pepper to taste

Preparation:

Set your oven to preheat at 350 degrees. Line two baking trays with baking paper and set aside. Take a large saucepan and heat some olive oil in it over medium heat.

Add the shallots and sauté them for 2 to 3 minutes or until they start to soften and go transparent. Add the garlic and mushroom stems and sauté for 4 to 5 minutes. Season with salt, pepper and paprika and set aside.

Take the mushroom caps and brush olive oil on the tops. Turn them over to make them look like bowls and spoon some of the garlic stuffing inside it. Fill all the mushrooms and place them on the baking tray.

Gently, slide the baking tray into the oven, to prevent the mushrooms from falling over. Let them bake in the oven for 10 to 15 minutes or until the mushrooms look cooked to you. Let them cool slightly before serving.

Nutrition information per serving: Kcal: 282 Protein: 11.7g, Carbs: 26.4g, Fats: 14.7g

29. Coconut and curry side dish

Ingredients:

2 cups of pumpkin puree

1 cup of vegetable broth

1 cup of coconut milk

½ tbsp of curry powder

¼ tsp of ground tumeric

2 tsp of masala

Salt and pepper to taste

1 tsp of minced garlic

½ onion, sliced

3 carrots, sliced

1 medium sweet potato, peeled and sliced

Preparation:

Add sliced sweet potato, coconut milk, pure, stock, curry, rest of seasonings and ingredients in a medium pot and stir well. Cook for about 30 minutes on low temperature. Serve with gluten free rice or noodles.

Nutrition information per serving: Kcal: 401 Protein:3.4g, Carbs: 32.5g, Fats: 28.7g

30. Baked Eggs and Prosciutto in Portobello Mushrooms

Ingredients:

6 mushroom caps (Portobello, cleaned, de-stemmed, scraped gills)

6 strips of Prosciutto

6 eggs

1 teaspoon of fresh parsley, chopped

3 tablespoons of olive oil

salt and pepper to taste

Preparation:

Your mushroom caps should be cleaned and cut into small bowl-like shapes. Take the caps and apply some olive oil on the outside to cook them easily and so that they will not stick to the baking sheet.

Line a baking tray with some baking paper before putting the mushroom caps on them. Take a slice of prosciutto and stuff it inside the mushroom cap. Make sure the slices fits neatly inside it.

Once you have stuffed all your mushroom caps with prosciutto, set them aside. Crack an egg into a small bowl and carefully, slide the egg inside the prosciutto stuffed mushroom cap. This step may take some time since the egg yolk can make the mushroom over-turn or spill out.

Once all the eggs are in the mushroom caps, season with some salt, parsley and pepper. Be careful of the salt since prosciutto is a rather salty meat and adding extra salt might make increase the saltiness of the dish.

Once you have seasoned everything, slide the baking tray extremely carefully into the oven. Be gentle to avoid overturning any mushroom caps. Once they're inside, let them cook for 30 minutes or until you feel the mushroom cap and egg are cooked to your liking.

Let them cool a bit before you take them out of the oven.

Nutrition information per serving: Kcal: 126 Protein: 12.6g, Carbs: 1.2g, Fats: 8.1g

31. Super food mix

Ingredients:

2 cups of almonds

1 cup of pumpkin seeds

1 cup of sunflower seeds

1 cup of flaked coconuts

¼ cup of Chia seeds

1 tablespoon of vanilla, grounded

1 ½ tablespoon of orange zest

½ cup of maple syrup

¼ cup of olive oil

¼ cup of apple butter

1 cup of apricots, dried and chopped

Preparation:

Preheat your oven at 275oF. Pulse the almonds in your food processor until they have been chopped a bit. Take a large bowl and add the almonds, pumpkin seeds, sunflower seeds, chia seeds, coconut flakes, orange zest, maple syrup, olive oil and apple butter.

Stir until the mixture is combined into a sticky, chunky batter. Take two baking trays and add some baking sheets to them. Pour the chunky mixture on to the sheets and flatten it a bit.

Bake them for 30 minutes in the oven or until it is golden brown. Make sure to check after every 10 minutes and give it a stir to prevent it from sticking. Take them out, add the apricots and let the granola cool off.

Nutrition information per serving: Kcal: 172 Protein: 7g, Carbs: 8.5g, Fats: 14 g

32. Vegetables get-away

Ingredients:

1 tomato

A handful of spinach

1 cup of water

1 tbsp of raw honey

A dash of sea salt

1 baby cucumber

Half of papaya

Preparation:

Peel the papaya and get rid of the cord. Chop the papaya into thin slices. Slice the cucumber with the skin on into thin slices. Add the cucumber slices, papaya slices, spinach, honey, tomato and salt to it. Blend for about 5 minutes and serve fresh.

Nutrition information per serving: Kcal: 280 Protein: 1.1g, Carbs: 8.4g, Fats: 28g

33. Mushroom tomato with onion gravy

Ingredients:

1 pound mushroom

½ cup of water

8 onions, chopped

4 tomatoes, chopped

3 red chilies, chopped

1 tsp of ginger

2 green chilies, chopped

1 tsp garlic

2 tbsp of olive oil

Fresh parsley

Salt and pepper to taste

Preparation:

In a non-stick frying pan, heat your olive oil. Throw in the chopped onion, and fry them for nearly 3 minutes or until they are brown. Throw in the mushrooms and fry for 5 minutes. Add the chilies, and the spices. Season with salt and pepper. Toss for about 4 minutes more and sprinkle the parsley.

Serve hot.

Nutrition information per serving: Kcal: 100 Protein: 3.6g, Carbs: 24g, Fats: 1.2g

34. Butternut squash with vegetables

Ingredients:

1 butternut squash, peeled, corded

4 carrots

1 pumpkin, peeled, corded

4 onions, chopped

2 tbsp of ginger garlic paste

1 tsp of cumin paste

Fresh coriander, chopped

6 cups of vegetable broth

1 tsp of pepper

2 green chilies, chopped

2 tbsp of olive oil

1 tsp of sea salt

Preparation:

Cut all the vegetables in a similar size in order to get good visual and also it would help to cook the vegetables evenly. Now in a slow cooker, add the oil and the vegetables. Add the chilies, pastes and season with salt and pepper. Pour in the broth and give it a good stir. Cover with the lid and turn the heat to low. Cook for about 3 hours and serve hot.

Nutrition information per serving: Kcal: 103 Protein: 4.3g, Carbs: 12g, Fats: 6.3g

35. Tomato and mushroom gluten-free pasta

Ingredients:

1 cup of zucchini noodle

2 tbsp of olive oil

1 cup of button mushroom, chopped

4 onions, diced

4 tomatoes, chopped

Salt to taste

Fresh parsley

Preparation:

Cook the zucchini noodle in hot water for about 5-6 minutes. Once done, drain and set aside for now. mIn a pan heat the oil and fry the onions brown. Throw in the mushroom and toss for 5 minutes. Add the tomatoes and fry them for 3 minutes. Season with salt and toss for just a minute. Plate up by adding the tomato mushroom mix on top of the boiled zucchini.

Garnish with fresh parsley.

Nutrition information per serving: Kcal: 145 Protein: 4.2g, Carbs: 31.4g, Fats: 11.2g

36. Brussels sprouts in coconut gravy

Ingredients:

1 pound of Brussels sprout

Fresh coriander

2 cup of coconut milk

4 onions, chopped

1 tbsp of olive oil

Salt and pepper to taste

½ cup of cashew paste

Preparation:

In a skillet heat the olive oil and throw in the onions. Fry for a minute and add the Brussels sprouts. Stir for about 5 minutes and then add the cashew paste to it. Toss for 2 minutes and then add the coconut milk. Season with salt and pepper. Check the consistency of the gravy and then reduce the heat. If you wish to make it creamy, add more cashew paste.

Serve with the coriander on top.

Nutrition information per serving: Kcal: 762 Protein: 19.3g, Carbs: 94.5g, Fats: 35.9g

37. Glazed Pumpkin Donuts

Ingredients:

Donuts:

2 cups almond flour

1 ½ tsp of baking powder

¼ cup of milk

1 ½ tsp of pumpkin pie spice

½ tsp of salt

¼ tsp of baking soda

1 cup of pumpkin puree

4 tbsp of agave nectar

2 whole eggs

¼ cup of butter, softened

Glaze:

2 tbsp water

¼ cup almond butter, melted

½ cup of sucanat

1 tsp vanilla extract

Preparation:

Preheat your oven to 325 degrees. In a baking sheet arrange the parchment paper and set aside for now. Take a large mixing bowl, and combine the flour with agave nectar. Gradually add the baking soda, baking powder, pumpkin pie spice and salt. Mix well and then pour the milk into the middle. Crack the eggs to the mixture and whisk well using a hand whisk. Add the softened butter to it following by the pumpkin puree. Now switch to electric beater and beat the mixture until the mix forms fine sticky dough. Transfer the dough onto a plain clear surface and roll it out flat. Cut into donuts using donut cutter. Place the donuts onto the parchment paper and let it rise for 10 minutes. Now place the tray into the oven and bake for about 10 minutes. Meanwhile, prepare the glaze, in a bowl mix together vanilla extract. Add melted butter and some water to it. Mix using a whisk until the mixture becomes very smooth.

Now take the donuts out of the oven and dip them into the glaze.

Nutrition information per serving: Kcal: 361 Protein: 4.2g, Carbs: 39.5g, Fats: 22g

38. Carrot puree

Ingredients:

3 cup of coconut milk

2 tbsp of coconut flour

1 tsp of cinnamon

4 carrots, sliced

2 tbsp of almond butter

6 tbsp of raw honey

Preparation:

Melt the butter in a non-stick pan and throw in the carrots. Toss for about 5 minutes and add the cinnamon. Add in the milk and continuously stir for 20 minutes. Stir in the flour and the honey. Check the taste and the thickness, if you are okay with the consistency then take off the heat. Serve cold.

Nutrition information per serving: Kcal: 125 Protein: 1.9g, Carbs: 18.7g, Fats: 5.8g

39. Apple Turnovers

Ingredients:

1 tbsp almond milk

17 ounce frozen gluten free puff pastry sheets, thawed

2 tbsp of lemon juice

2 tbsp of butter

4 apples

4 cups of water

1 cup of sugar

1 tbsp of water

1 tsp of ground cinnamon

1 cup of brown sugar

1 tsp of vanilla extract

Preparation:

Start by preheating your oven to 400 degrees. In a large bowl let the lemon soak into 4 cups of water and set aside for now. Peel the apples and take the cord out. Slice them into thin pieces and add them to the water. Drain well and rinse. In a non-stick pan, melt the butter. Add the apple slices and toss it for about 2-3 minutes. Now add that to the pan and toss for about 2 minutes. Take the pan off the stove. In a plain surface, unfold the pastry. Cut it into 4 squares. Fill the middle of those squares with the apple mixture. Now take the edges of each square and pull them in the center. It would create a triangle shape. Once done with all, place them onto a baking tray. Bake for about 25 minutes in the preheated oven.

Meanwhile prepare the glaze by mixing together the milk with the vanilla. Add sugar with it.

Take the apple turnovers out of the oven and brush the top with the glaze.

Serve warm or cold.

Nutrition information per serving: Kcal: 286 Protein: 3.1g, Carbs: 35.8g, Fats: 14.8g

40. Almond Egg Farinata

Ingredients:

1 cup of almond flour

4 onions, chopped

2 organic eggs

2 red chilies, chopped

1 tsp of pepper

Fresh mint

2 green chilies, chopped

1 tsp of cumin

Salt to taste

Preparation:

Preheat the oven to 350 degrees. In a large mixing bowl, throw in the almond flour, onions, and red chilies. Whisk in the eggs and mix until the mixture is smooth. Sprinkle the cumin, pepper and salt to it. Give it a good stir. Place in a greased baking dish and bake 10 minutes. Serve hot.

Nutrition information per serving: Kcal: 150 Protein: 2g, Carbs: 20g, Fats: 9g

41. Rice with tumeric

Ingredients

1 ½ cups Long Grain Rice

2 cups of vegetable broth (Your choice)

1 teaspoon of turmeric powder

1 diced yellow onion

1 tablespoon extra-virgin coconut oil

1 inch diced fresh ginger

2 minced garlic cloves

½ teaspoon cumin seed

Instructions

Pour the oil in a frying pan and put over high heat. Add the onion to the oil and sauté it till it is completely transparent. Then, put in the garlic and ginger. Keep sautéing for 4 minutes or so.

Combine the rice in the mixture. Pour the cumin seed on the rice and let them fry for around 5 minutes.

Sprinkle the turmeric on top. Toss the rice so that the color and flavour of the turmeric is evenly distributed.

Take a deep pot and pour in the broth you have selected.

Add the rice to the broth and bring it to a boil. Turn the heat down and leave the rice on to cook for another 15 or so minutes. Make sure the broth has been absorbed completely. Also, the rice should have softened before you remove it from the stove.

If you feel the rice hasn't cooked properly, you can add more broth to it and boil again.

Nutrition information per serving: Kcal: 145 Protein: 2.7g, Carbs: 28.3g, Fats: 2.1g

42. Vegetarian rice couscous

Ingredients:

1 cup of brown rice, cooked

2 large carrots

½ tsp of dried rosemary

10 green olives, pitted

1 tbsp of lemon juice

1 tbsp of orange juice

1 tbsp of orange zest

4 tbsp of olive oil

½ tsp of salt

Preparation:

Wash and peel carrots. Cut into thin slices. Heat up 2 tbsp of olive oil in a large pan over medium heat. Add carrots and cook, stirring constantly. It should be tender after about 10-15 minutes. Add rosemary, olives and orange juice. Mix well. Continue to cook and stir occasionally.

Combine lemon juice with 1 cup of water. Add this mixture to a saucepan and mix with 2 tbsp of olive oil, orange zest and salt. Allow it to boil and add rice. Remove from heat and allow it to stand for about 15 minutes.

Pour these two mixtures into a large bowl and mix well with a tablespoon.

Nutrition information per serving: Kcal: 220 Protein: 6.6g, Carbs: 40.4g, Fats: 4.3g

43. Grilled avocado in curry sauce

Ingredients:

1 large avocado, chopped

¼ cup of water

1 tbsp of ground curry

2 tbsp of olive oil

1 tsp of tomato sauce

1 tsp of chopped parsley

¼ tsp of red pepper

¼ tsp of sea salt

Preparation:

Heat up olive oil in a large saucepan, over a medium temperature. In a small bowl, combine ground curry, tomato sauce, chopped parsley, red pepper and sea salt. Add water and cook for about 5 minutes, over a medium temperature. Add chopped avocado, stir well and cook for another few minutes, until all the liquid evaporates. Turn off the heat and cover. Let it stand for about 15-20 minutes before serving.

Nutrition information per serving: Kcal: 229 Protein: 4.9g, Carbs: 13.3g, Fats: 20g

44. Fried vegetables with cottage cheese

Ingredients:

½ cup of cottage cheese

1 small onion

1 small carrot

1 small tomato

2 medium red peppers

salt to taste

1 tbsp of olive oil

Preparation:

Wash and pat dry the vegetables using a kitchen paper. Cut into thin slices or strips. Heat up the olive oil over a medium temperature and fry the vegetables for about 10 minutes, stirring constantly. Add salt and mix well. You want to wait until the vegetables soften, then add soft cottage cheese. Stir well. Fry for another 2-3 minutes. Remove from the heat and serve.

Nutrition information per serving: Kcal: 130 Protein: 8.4g, Carbs: 9.1g, Fats: 7.1g

45. Creamy leek

Ingredients:

2 cups of trimmed leeks

1 cup of low-fat cream

½ cup of cottage cheese

olive oil

thyme leaves for decoration

salt and red pepper to taste

Preparation:

Cut the leeks into small pieces and wash it under cold water, day before serving. Leave it overnight in a plastic bag.

Heat the oil in a large pan, over a medium temperature. Add cottage cheese and cream and fry for about 15 minutes. Add leaks, mix well and fry for another 10 minutes on a low temperature. Remove from the saucepan and allow it to cool. Decorate with thyme leaves. Add salt and pepper to taste.

Nutrition information per serving: Kcal: 151 Protein: 7.4g, Carbs: 10.2g, Fats: 9.7g

46. Eggplant casserole

Ingredients:

2 large eggplants

1 cup of gorgonzona cheese, melted

1 medium onion

2 tbsp of oil

¼ tsp of pepper

2 small tomatoes

1 tbsp of dried parsley

½ cup of cottage cheese

3 tbsp of buckwheat crumbs

1 cup of milk

½ cup of cream

Preparation:

Grease the baking pan with oil. Preheat the oven at 350 degrees. Peel the eggplants and cut them lengthwise into thin slices. Layer eggplant slices in a baking pan. Peel and cut the onion and tomatoes into thin slices. Make another layer in a baking pan. Spread the melted gorgonzola on top.

Combine buckwheat crumbs with milk, cottage cheese, cream, parsley and pepper in a large bowl. Whisk well until smooth mixture. Pour this mixture on top of your casserole and bake for about 20 minutes.

Cut into 6 equal pieces and serve.

Nutrition information per serving: Kcal: 200 Protein: 4g, Carbs: 15.5g, Fats: 14.8g

47. Vegetarian burritos

Ingredients:

1 cup of rice, cooked

1 sweet potato, cooked and chopped into small cubes

1 cup of cottage cheese

½ cup of chopped onions

1 tsp of ground red pepper

1 tsp of chili powder

6 whole grain, gluten-free tortillas

Preparation:

Combine sweet potato cubes with ground red pepper, chili powder and onions in a frying pan. Stir well for 15 minutes on a low temperature. Remove from the heat.

Mix cottage cheese with cooked rice in a blender. Mix well for about 30 seconds. Add the cottage cheese mixture to the sweet potato. Divide this mixture into 6 equal pieces and spread over tortillas. Wrap and serve.

Nutrition information per serving: Kcal: 461 Protein: 24.1g, Carbs: 130g, Fats: 19.1g

ADDITIONAL TITLES FROM THIS AUTHOR

70 Effective Meal Recipes to Prevent and Solve Being Overweight: Burn Fat Fast by Using Proper Dieting and Smart Nutrition

By

Joe Correa CSN

48 Acne Solving Meal Recipes: The Fast and Natural Path to Fixing Your Acne Problems in Less Than 10 Days!

By

Joe Correa CSN

41 Alzheimer's Preventing Meal Recipes: Reduce or Eliminate Your Alzheimer's Condition in 30 Days or Less!

By

Joe Correa CSN

70 Effective Breast Cancer Meal Recipes: Prevent and Fight Breast Cancer with Smart Nutrition and Powerful Foods

By

Joe Correa CSN

www.ingramcontent.com/pod-product-compliance
Lightning Source LLC
Chambersburg PA
CBHW052036070526
44584CB00016B/2072